# TEN
## *Keys*
### to
# AVOID
# DEBT

*The Devils Evil*
*Borrowing Trap*

PHYLLIS TUFTS HIGHTOWER

**author**HOUSE®

*AuthorHouse™*
*1663 Liberty Drive*
*Bloomington, IN 47403*
*www.authorhouse.com*
*Phone: 833-262-8899*

*Published by Authorhouse 10/24/2022*

*ISBN: 978-1-6655-7390-0 (sc)*
*ISBN: 978-1-6655-7078-7 (e)*

*Library of Congress Control Number: 2022919733*

*Print information available on the last page.*

*This book is printed on acid-free paper.*

*Because of the dynamic nature of the Internet, any web addresses or links contained in this book may have changed since publication and may no longer be valid. The views expressed in this work are solely those of the author and do not necessarily reflect the views of the publisher, and the publisher hereby disclaims any responsibility for them.*

# CONTENTS

# DEDICATION

In memory of my parents

The late Rev. Cornelius and Annie Mae Tufts, the people who first loved nurtured me and laid the foundation for my Christian Faith. I acknowledge and remember them for helping to mold me into the Christ centered person that I am today. I am forever grateful for the solid spiritual training that has brought me this far.

# INTRODUCTION

## *My Accidental Journey to Saving Money*

The watch was on display at the drugstore in our town. It was a Disney *Cinderella* watch, and at eight years old, I thought it was beautiful. To say that I wanted that watch would be an understatement. The watch was nine dollars, and though that doesn't sound like much, to me back then, it might as well have been a thousand dollars and not something that I could have asked my parents for. But what I did not know was that my change collection, mostly pennies which I carried around in my little purse, nearly added up to the amount of the watch. I simply left the store and continued to save up, and within a short time, I was able to go back in and buy that watch. You can't imagine the feeling of accomplishment I had as we drove home with that watch on my wrist.

In this way, you could say I learned a valuable, early lesson quite by accident. I learned that you could delay gratification and save money when you wanted to buy something. I could have looked at the watch, looked at my money purse, realized I didn't quite have enough, and then started looking around for cheaper items to spend my money on. Maybe I could have even asked to borrow a little from my parents to buy the watch. Then, the lesson would have been a completely different one. I would have learned to be in debt! Thank God that isn't what happened.

Later in life, when I was in college, I took that lesson and saved up $1000 cash to buy a car from a family member. The car faithfully transported me from point A to point B for many years after graduation and was a huge blessing, ushering me into early adulthood.

And finally, I continued to apply these lessons and was able to retire earlier than the average person. In fact, the average person has trouble retiring at all, because they have lived the opposite way. They may have been the little girl or boy who learned to borrow, to gain instant gratification, to buy now, pay later for liabilities that would keep them shackled for life. I was blessed to "accidentally" come by the skill of saving for what was important to me, thinking long term and delaying gratification. If that wasn't you, this book is for you. You may think it is too late, but it is never too late to change your life. If you are ready, keep reading.

# What is Debt?

*The first key is to know what debt is:*
*The Devil's Borrowing Trap*

Have you ever considered what it would be like to go to prison? Maybe you've watched a television show or a movie about prison, and have shuttered at the idea of being locked up for life in that environment. For those of you unfortunate enough to have been to prison, I doubt you would say that you want to go back for a sentence of five, ten, fifteen years, or even life.

Getting into debt is very much a prison sentence. It's easy for most of us to grasp how horrible it is to be incarcerated and lose freedom, but so many people fail to realize how having large amounts of debt is bondage, literally trapping people until it is paid. In the old days, there was something called debtor's prison, where someone was kept when they couldn't pay their debts. This provides a clearer picture of debt as a prison.

An example of this in the Bible is found in 2 Kings 4:1-7

> Now the wife of one of the sons of the prophets cried to Elisha, "Your servant my husband is dead, and you know that your servant feared the Lord, but **the creditor has come to take my two children to be his slaves**." 2 And Elisha said to her, "What shall I do for you? Tell me; what have you in the house?" And she said, "Your servant has nothing in the house except a jar of oil." 3 Then he said, "Go outside, borrow vessels from all your neighbors, empty vessels and not too few. 4 Then go in and shut the door behind yourself and your sons and pour into all these vessels. And when one is full, set it aside." 5 So she went from him and shut the door behind herself and her sons. And as she poured they brought the vessels to her. 6 When the vessels were full, she said to her son, "Bring me another vessel." And he said to her, "There is not another." Then the oil stopped flowing. 7 She came and told the man of God, and he said, "Go, sell the oil and pay your debts, and you and your sons can live on the rest." (ESV emphasis added)

This short passage teaches us a great deal. A man had creditors with no plan to pay it off if he died. He was owned by his creditors, and by extension, we see that his wife and children were owned. As a result, the creditors had the right to take the children in payment for the debt. We have a greater revelation today of the difference between people and property, but back then, most of humanity made no such distinction.

Even today, it feels almost the same. If you are in debt, you are in a trap, you are a slave to the lender. Proverbs 22:7 tells us, "The rich rule over the poor, and the borrower is slave to the lender" (NIV). God never intended for His people to be borrowers. If you survey the whole of Scripture, it shows that borrowing in and of itself is not *wrong*. God borrowed the womb of Mary. He borrowed a little Boys lunch, a boat from Peter and Andrew. And although he did not need it long he borrowed a tomb. Point is that when God borrows from us he always gives it back with increase and this is a stewardship principle to explore in chapter 10. If you have some reason to buy someone's money now with more money you are going to pay later, then by agreement, that is okay. But what God shows us is that it is far better to be the lender in that situation. The borrower is simply not free. It is not God's best.

The acronym I'll use throughout this book for Debt, is the **D**evil's **E**vil **B**orrowing **T**rap. It is rare for someone to borrow without borrowing becoming a habit. When you are in the habit of borrowing, you are caught in a trap. Satan likes to see you poor and in bondage. He loves to put you in situations where you are forced to make poor decisions that you might not have made if you were free.

But God never intended for His people to be caught in the borrowing trap, and He established specific, actionable principles to avoid this pitfall. Looking back at the widow's pot of oil, when she was in trouble, she looked for help from God by seeking help from His prophet. The prophet's solution began with a question. What do you have that is valuable? She said "nothing". But she didn't have "nothing", she had some oil. In chapters 6 and 10, and also sprinkled throughout the whole book, this principle will be revisited as the principle of stewardship. God has given all of us *something*, even if it seems like a small amount. We always have somewhere to start when it comes to faithfulness. That is a sure antidote for avoiding the debt trap.

Once Elisha shows the woman that she does have *something,* we see God get to work blessing her as she puts her meager ration of oil to work. There is a powerful principle there, but I do not want to get ahead of myself.

Simply put, if you are in debt, you are in bondage. To get out of bondage, the Devil's Evil Borrowing Trap, you must get out of debt. Once you are out of debt, you are free to soar.

## Good Debt vs. Bad Debt

A strong biblical case can be made for the idea that there is no such thing as "good debt." But logic tells us that all debt is not created equal. What most would consider "good debt" is the kind of debt that is productive. When you buy a house and take out a mortgage with a low interest rate, that could be considered good debt. You will likely pay less for a mortgage payment than you would pay in rent on the same property, *and* at the end of 15 or 30 years, you will own the property.

Another example might be a business loan or a student loan that is an investment in your future earning potential. If you could get a small business loan to start an enterprise that pays off the loan and continues to provide a profit, then you could make a case that it is a good debt. If you get a student loan for an education that will allow you to get a well paying job at the end of it, you can pay off the student loan later, and then continue saving money, working with the skills you acquired in school.

However, those debts are not fool-proof. Many have gotten into trouble buying a house they couldn't afford in a real estate market that went down. Then, a good debt becomes a bad debt. Considering that the appreciation on real estate is historically lower than other investments like mutual funds, a home can also become a bad debt when it loses value and you can't get out from under it.

The same applies to business and education loans. A business may very well not make it. In fact, that is statistically what happens. Most businesses fail within a few years. Often it is *because* of the debt incurred to start. It's much better if you can fund a business with cash so that interest payments are not eating up precious profits. And many people take out student loans and don't finish college. No degree, high debt. Or they go to a school with high tuition and major in something that doesn't pay well. I've seen many get $180,000 degrees in something like social work, which will not pay them enough to make the minimum loan payments due after graduation. That's a bad debt. That's bondage.

Why not look for ways to live outside any debt trap? Why not look for ways to buy homes, start businesses, and go to college without using debt? Thousands of people do it, and so can you. The rest of this book will help you do that.

CHAPTER 2

# *Two Economies in Opposition*

Ever since the fall of humanity in the garden of Eden, there have been two opposing kingdoms. When our first father and mother handed the world over to the serpent by their rebellion towards their Father's command, they gave the evil one mostly free reign. That is, until the promised Messiah came and announced the dramatic invasion of the kingdom of God into the world of darkness.

"The people living in darkness have seen a great light; on those living in the land of the shadow of death a light has dawned" (Mt 4:16 NIV).

Now, while the world is still fallen and will be until the second coming of Christ, there has been an in-breaking of the heavenly kingdom. Jesus showed that the reality of the kingdom of God was both "already" and "not yet." While people are still sick in the fallen world today, sometimes they get healed through prayer. This is one example of the future kingdom of God breaking into the current kingdom of Satan, the Light of the World breaking into the darkness. The fact that sometimes people do not get healed is evidence that we are in a world where there is still darkness. When Christ returns, He will eradicate the darkness once and for all. But until then, we live among two opposing kingdoms. We pray for victory for the kingdom of God when we pray as Christ taught us, "Thy will be done on earth *as it is in heaven*" (Mt 6:10). When God's will is done everywhere on earth as it is in heaven, the darkness will have ceased. Until then we live in a spiritual battle.

This also means that we live amidst two opposing economies, the world's economy versus God's economy. In the world's economy, money is here to buy happiness, status, comfort, and anything else that one may want to replace God with. The Bible calls these things idols when they are used to fill the void in our heart that is meant to be filled with a relationship with our Creator. In the world's economy, since the goal is the outcome, people use debt to reach the outcome. I may not have any money, but if I can borrow it, I can get things *now* that I cannot afford. The world's economy runs on discontent and it runs on debt. To play in the world's economy is to get into a hole that is impossible to get out of. That is, it is impossible to get out of until we switch economies.

To get out of the debt-hole, the Devil's Evil Borrowing Trap, we must refuse to operate by the world's economy. The only way to do that is to operate in God's economy. In this economy, we understand tithing, saving, giving above our tithe, living in abundance, buying things we love *when* we have given and saved.

## Tithing

Tithing is a biblical principle, but it is not commanded in the New Testament. Even so, many faithful Christians have founding tithing, the giving of 10% of our gross income, to be a wonderful discipline to protect our hearts against the love of money, and to fund the work of Jesus' Church in the world. Without going to every place in the law where tithing is commanded (and no, Christians are not under Old Testament law), I want to go back *before* the law to show the principle observed.

Abraham prospered as he obeyed God and lived according to God's ways. After he had won a victory over some enemy nations in order to rescue his nephew, Lot, Abraham returned home. On the way, he met a mysterious man named Melchizedek.

> 18 And Melchizedek, the king of Salem and a priest of God Most High, brought Abram some bread and wine. 19 Melchizedek blessed Abram with this blessing:
>
> "Blessed be Abram by God Most High,
>     Creator of heaven and earth.
> 20 And blessed be God Most High,
>     who has defeated your enemies for you."
> Then Abram gave Melchizedek a tenth of all the goods he had recovered. (Gen 14:18-20)

Melchizedek is thought by some to be God the Son. Others think he is merely a priest of God, but either way, there was something in Abraham that made him think he should give God's representative a tithe of all he had taken. So tithing was before the law.

Why tithe? Why give anything for that matter? Because Jesus said that when we give, we store up treasure in heaven (Mt 6:20). Paul mentioned this as well to the Philippian church. In Philippians 4:17 he said, "Not that I seek the gift, but I seek the fruit that increases to your credit" (ESV). Paul was thanking them for the gift they had sent him. He said the fruit of that giving goes on their account. One reason that debt is so bad is that it causes you not to save. If you don't save, you cannot get ahead financially. So we must save, especially for our later retirement years. But even more importantly, we must save for our eternal life. If having resources is important in later life on earth, it is infinitely more important for eternal life in heaven.

Obviously there is great mystery around the nature of eternal life. What will it be like? One thing we know is that if we give on earth there is an account on which our giving shows up for use there. Unlike our earthly bank accounts, which today only pay .025 percent interest, our heavenly accounts pay an infinitely high interest rate!

We are talking about the economy of the kingdom of God versus the economy of the kingdom of darkness. Getting into debt is playing the Devil's game. Staying out of debt is the start of living in the kingdom economy, but giving generously is the ultimate end.

Like Abraham and the Israelites, learn to tithe first on your gross income. Why? Because this is your "firstfruits". Proverbs 3:9 says, "Honor the Lord with your wealth, with the firstfruits of all your crops" (NIV).

## What About This Life?

Proverbs 11:24 says, "There is the one who [generously] scatters [abroad], and yet increases all the more; And there is the one who withholds what is justly due, but it results only in want and poverty" (AMP).

In general, especially if one reads Proverbs, it is clear that what goes for eternal life goes for life on this earth. But sometimes, especially noticeable in books like Ecclesiastes or Job, bad things happen that don't seem to fit that principle.

Sometimes bad things just happen as a result of the fact the world is fallen. We live in a strange time in the history of creation where, for those of us living on earth, we are at an *in-between* time, where the kingdom of God has broken into the present life through the coming of Christ. And when He came, He brought the power of this future Kingdom of God where God's will is done "on earth as it is in heaven." But it did not fully come. He also said the kingdom was still *coming*. We know from the New Testament that it will fully come when Christ returns, but in this life, the kingdom of darkness still has some power. We live among these opposing kingdoms, and we seek to live the Kingdom of God life as much as we possibly can by faith.

Tithing, giving, serving, living in righteousness are all Kingdom of God ways to live, that is, living as lights in the darkness. When it comes to finances, we seek to live out the Kingdom of God economy as opposed to the kingdom of darkness, or the world's economy. The rest of the chapters will show how.

CHAPTER

3

# *How the Prosperity Gospel Left God's People in Debt*

There's no doubt that the many needs we face every day can leave everyone, including Christians, swimming in an ocean of bills and wondering if they will ever catch up. Of course, we all look for a source of income that will help us maintain a place to live, put food on the table, and have enough clothing to stay comfortable.

But what does it take to make sure you stay afloat? Many of us find ourselves in debt due to an inability to make ends meet. Beyond that, you may want to provide things like dance lessons or team jerseys for your kids' sports activities. Or maybe you just want to take your family on a nice vacation. These aren't bad things, but affording them without too much trouble can sometimes seem like an unreachable dream.

These days, the prosperity gospel has positioned itself as a source of hope and inspiration for many Christians with financial worries. This is the belief that God will reward the greater faith of Christians with excellent health and wealth. *And the more money you donate to His ministry, the more you will be paid back in material blessings.*

The prosperity gospel has uplifted many Christians while being highly criticized by others. Although it provides some value, it has led many to make unwise decisions. As with anything else, you'll need to exercise wisdom and caution, rather than emotional excitement, when making financial choices.

## *Prosperity and Hope*

Let's begin by talking about what the prosperity gospel gets right.

First of all, it's important to keep in mind that humans are designed to be motivated by hope. Positive characteristics like hard work and responsibility are driven by our belief that we can have more resources and esteem if we continue to do what is right in the face of adversity.

Many psychologists note the importance of hope in helping us to overcome stress and anxiety. It's critical to our long-term happiness as well as our mental health. A wellspring of it can inspire us to achieve high-quality goals that require struggles, lessons, and inevitable disappointments along the way.

Most lives are a continual push and pull of positive and negative events. Hope is what allows us to live meaningfully in balance no matter what happens.

Of course, the Bible gives us more reason to hope than anything else does. Titus 1:2 reminds Christians that we trust "in the hope of eternal life, which God, who never lies, promised before the ages began" (ESV.)

Our greatest problem, which is that of the sin that separates us from an eternally good and holy God, has been eliminated through the work of His Son on the cross. Free from this burden, we can begin pursuing enterprises that please Him.

Yet the Bible also gives us some reason to believe that our commitment to Him will bring hope for blessings in this present life.

For example, Psalm 1 verses 1–3 tells us that

> Blessed is the one who walks not in the counsel of the wicked, nor stands in the way of sinners, nor sits in the seat of scoffers; but His delight is in the law of the Lord, and on His law, he meditates day and night. He is like a tree planted by streams of water that yields its fruit in season, and its leaf does not wither. In all that he does, he prospers. (ESV)

Here we see that we can have faith that our obedience to the Lord will yield good things. If we refuse to take part in the mocking, laziness, and addictive sins that others indulge in, we will be blessed.

Much of this blessing is spiritual and circumstantial rather than financial. For example, your family will stay intact if you continue to work hard and avoid traps like adultery or anger. You will be recognized by your employer if you aren't gossiping in the workplace. You'll continue to reap peace if you are looking to God for your strength rather than to the fleeting pleasures of sin.

Yet some of these blessings can also relate to our finances. For example, a faithful husband and father may be motivated to start a business that glorifies God. If he does so with thoughtful planning and respect for biblical principles, his business can be rewarded with great success.

Another thing that the prosperity gospel encourages is the idea of continuing to hope in the midst of difficult circumstances.

Hebrews 11:1 tells us that "Now faith is the assurance of things hoped for, the conviction of things not seen"(ESV).

It's so easy for individuals who are facing a difficult state of affairs to become discouraged. This can lead to things like depression, addiction, and even problems with daily functioning. Of course, this negative thinking can make circumstances even worse. The prosperity gospel encourages us to have faith in the future even if we can't see it yet. This is a much-needed word for those who are struggling.

## *The Problem with Prosperity Preaching*

In spite of its positive attributes, however, the prosperity gospel has misled many Christians.

The teachings of some prosperity preachers, for example, have led many Christ-followers to believe that suffering and self-denial are not a normal part of the life of faith.

Traditionally, the means for achieving financial security for yourself and your family involved such things as sacrificing. You shouldn't be purchasing things you can't afford. You may need to be coupon-clipping, re-using, and thrift-store shopping in order to put food on tables and clothes on backs. If you are diligent, you can eventually get the things you'd really like to have.

The messages of many preachers, however, may lead one to believe that their real problem is simply a lack of sufficient faith. If we believed enough, we would enjoy plenty. Our experience of lack of funds or things not going our way isn't natural to the Christian walk.

This has led to many believers thinking that they simply need to take more "steps of faith" *by giving more to a particular ministry* or buying things as though they already had the money. The real result is additional debt, struggle, and hardship.

Another large problem with prosperity preaching is that it places Christians at the center of the walk of faith rather than our Savior. True Christ-followers know that the only reason we can hope for our eternal home is that a holy Jesus took our place on the cross, and not because we have such impressive faith.

Other scholars have criticized the lack of seriousness given to Christian faith when one focuses on a prosperity message. This can be a fair judgment when one considers the shallow walk of many who focus on their physical well-being rather than their salvation when it comes to spiritual matters.

It's important to remember that, as with anything else in life, balance is key. Many seeking more financial security for their families find their inspiration in the message of Scripture. It's important, however, to remember that it is God we should be seeking first, rather than His blessings.

## Seek His Face and Not His Hand

"Seeking God's hand and not His face" is an expression that is often used by Christians to describe a focus on what God can give us, rather than who He is.

Those who are truly blessed know the key is in seeking God Himself rather than other gifts we might want from Him. This requires some discipline initially.

For example, did you know that gratitude is critical for mental health? If you are grateful, you will have a much easier time enjoying your life and building strong relationships.

One way to keep your mind on your Savior rather than what you want is to keep a "gratitude journal" where you write down what you are thankful for each day. Did you have enough to eat and a way to get to work? Do you have a bed to sleep in and a coat in the winter?

We don't need to have a lot to know that God loves us. Remind yourself each day of how fortunate you are that your Savior is meeting your basic needs.

In addition, now can be a great time to learn to rest simply in the peace of God Himself. Find time every day to study scripture and pray. Start your daily alone time with the Lord by adoring Him for who He is and what He has done, rather than furnishing Him with your list of needs. A season of struggle can be a time when God wants to prune you by developing a mature faith that isn't based on your circumstances.

Another great way to seek the face of your Savior is to give to others. It may seem counterproductive to spend your time helping someone else when you feel lacking in yourself. Yet this kind of work helps us to take the focus off of ourselves and turn our eyes to our Savior.

Can you dedicate one evening a week to helping at a homeless shelter, or donate a few dollars every month to support an orphan in a foreign country? Do you know of an extended family member or church attendant who could use a ride to work or a free babysitter?

It can often be difficult to motivate ourselves to serve when we can expect nothing in return. Yet Scripture reminds us that "Whoever is generous to the poor lends to the Lord, and He will repay him for his deed (Pr 19:17, ESV).

Helping others in need can remind us of just how blessed we truly are. If you are seeking the gifts of God in your life, begin by reminding yourself that He has already provided the greatest Blessing of all, and He has promised to supply all of your needs (Phil 4:19).

# Seek First the Kingdom

Many Christians are familiar with the popular Scripture "But seek first His kingdom and His righteousness, and all these things will be added to you" (Mt 6:33 ESV).

Seeking God first is a message about priority. If your number one concern is the kingdom of God, other blessings will eventually follow.

When we seek God first, we are always working for His kingdom. We want to know how we can serve Him and advance the Gospel. All of our activities, including those at work and home, center around our desire to see His kingdom glorified.

Seeking God first can supply a tremendous amount of emotional relief when we have uncertain moments. Many of us are tempted to worry or call a friend when we are fearful of something.

These solutions can help a bit, but they will never cure your problem. When you seek the Lord first, however, you are free to seek refuge in your Savior. He can comfort you, uplift you, and help you. And He can supply you with the wisdom you need to begin making smarter decisions.

## Start Seeking

Of course, devotional time with your Heavenly Father is critical to keeping your eyes on your Savior. You may have read some Bible verses hundreds of times, but there is always something new He can teach you.

Prayer is another integral part of your walk that is often neglected by many Christians. It helps us develop a meaningful relationship with God. If you don't currently start your day with prayer, resolve to make it a habit to open your heart to your Father every morning. Your prayer doesn't need to be lengthy, but it does need to be sincere.

Many of us begin praying by looking for a miracle. We have an immediate need or feel overwhelmed, and we know that only He can help us.

Yet prayer that is praise, and acknowledges God for all of His goodness, is critical as well. There is a need for worship in all of our hearts that can only be properly fulfilled by God. When we sinfully give this praise to other people or things, we will always be restless and unhappy.

Thank God for your victories and small triumphs, and invite Him to touch your life in the areas where you're vexed, including your finances. Once your heart is in a good place due to praise and thanksgiving, your need will seem less overwhelming.

Obeying God is another important facet of keeping Him first. If you are seeking God's blessing but still indulging in behavior and thoughts that contradict His Word, you're not going to see victory. Seeking God first means that you're going to follow His teachings even when it's difficult.

Serving in God's church and memorizing Scripture are also wonderful ways to give the Lord the priority He deserves. If you aren't a part of a small group or Bible study, don't hesitate to get involved. The right group of Christians will hold you accountable, encourage you, and provide biblical guidance.

## *Becoming a Good Steward*

A good steward is someone who wisely and faithfully manages whatever resources God has provided us with. It's someone who works hard, saves, and invests intelligently in the future.

Sometimes, the gifts we are called to look after aren't financial. Your family, for example, isn't a material blessing. Yet parents are called to "Train up a child in the way he should go, and when he is old he will not depart from it" (Pr 22:6).

A good parent knows that children trained in biblical principles from the beginning will honor them later on. Teaching them kindness, respect, and self-control is an important investment in the future of God's Kingdom.

We are also called to be good stewards of our spiritual gifts and talents. For example, you may have been born with wonderful musical ability. Wasting it will result in an unfulfilling life. Even singing in your church choir once a week can give you the confidence that you are using your gifts to advance the kingdom of God.

In addition, it's important to honor God with the words He gives us. Are you using your voice to encourage your brothers and sisters and spur them on toward obedience and good deeds? Or are you tearing those in your life down with your harsh criticism?

Of course, most people think of money when they hear the word "stewardship." This involves things like paying off and staying out of debt. It's also important to save for the future, including your retirement and children's education.

A good steward will make tithing a priority. They will think as far ahead as their grandchildren when planning for a financially stable future. This may require sacrifices such as going without luxuries or getting a second job.

The Bible tells us that "the plans of the diligent lead surely to abundance, but everyone who is hasty comes only to poverty" (Pr 21:5 ESV).

The investments you make with your time and money should never be based upon a whim or a scheme. If you aren't a savvy investor, seek godly counsel from someone who has expertise in that area. What is the best way to save for things like college? Can automated payments help you to avoid falling behind?

A wise steward knows what will reasonably be expected in the years ahead. They will make a financial plan and put away money each month that will help them reach their goals. Any business venture is guided by biblical principles and relies on the skills of hard-working, godly individuals for support.

The Bible promises that "Behold, my servant shall act wisely, and he shall be high and lifted up, and shall be exalted" (Isa 52:13 ESV).

Financial prudence never goes unrewarded. If you choose to honor God with your money, you will be highly esteemed.

## *Learning to Be Content*

Many Christians have a constant drive to succeed more than they have in the past. They are driven to go over and above, unwilling to stop pushing themselves to be and do better.

This desire is not wrong. In fact, the Bible tells us that "In toil there is profit, but mere talk leads only to poverty" (Pr 14:23 ESV).

If you want to succeed in life, you must be willing to put your oar in and row. Careful planning, deliberate action, and faithfulness are the key to your prosperity. You cannot spend your days complaining or hiding in your room with the covers over your head. Your time must be filled with hard work if you want to achieve your goals.

This does not mean, however, that we need to live in a state of constant vexation until we get the results we're looking for. This is not good for your mental or physical health. In fact, contentment will lead to peace of mind, positivity, and happiness that will make you more prepared to work in the direction of your dreams.

In Philippians 4:11-13, the author tells us that "Not that I am speaking of being in need, for I have learned in no matter what situation I am in to be content. I know how to be brought low, and I know how to abound. In every and any circumstance, I have learned the secret of facing plenty and hunger, abundance and need. I can do all things through Him who strengthens me" (ESV).

Paul is imploring us not to wait until all of our circumstances are to our liking to be happy. If we are hungry, tired, or in need, we can always feel blessed. The reason is because we can do everything through Christ, who is our constant source of strength.

## Finding Contentment

One of the best ways to learn contentment is to change the way you think and speak about your life. The Bible tells us that a man is what he thinks about (Pr 23:7).

What do you tell yourself about your circumstances? Do you complain inwardly about your lack of nice things or the condition of your home? Do you grumble to others about how you struggle to pay the bills?

Believe it or not, complaining can actually impact your physical, as well as emotional, health. It can make you more susceptible to things like diabetes, obesity, and heart disease. It can also damage your memory and even shorten your lifespan. In addition, complaining will have the unintended effect of making those around you negative, which will in turn impact you.

If you whine a lot inwardly or outwardly, it's time to change the channel in your mind. The wonderful news here is that you have the ability to control what you dwell on. When a negative thought enters your brain, you can train yourself to begin thinking about something else.

Did your child spill something on the floor? It's normal to be upset, but you want to be careful not to begin stewing in your frustration. Remind yourself about something fun you are looking forward to, such as a vacation or a day out. When you revisit the incident later, you'll wonder what you were so bothered about.

Another great way to practice contentment is to reign in your spending habits. It's easy to waste time getting drawn into the vortex of buying online, where you'll find plenty of things you didn't know you needed until you saw them. This can also be a temptation at big box stores, where a trip in for a gallon of milk will lead you past clothes, electronics, and decorations that can really draw you in.

You should always ask yourself if you need something before you buy it. If you really feel that the item would be a worthwhile addition to your life, give yourself some time to think about it. In a few days, you may not feel as strong a desire to make the purchase.

You'll also learn contentment by taking care of what God has already given you. Make sure you are eating right, sleeping well, and getting the proper amount of exercise. Dressing neatly doesn't require riches. You can find quality, well-fitting clothes at the right second-hand shop as long as you find the right one.

Keep your home clean and don't leave dirty dishes in the sink overnight. Get rid of things that aren't necessary so they don't clog up your mind. You will find that you can be content with very little as long as your surroundings are in order.

Of course, there are plenty of things in life that don't cost any money at all. Learning to plant your feet in these types of activities will go a long way toward helping you find contentment in your current financial position.

Would you enjoy taking out a book at your local library or going for a walk in the park? Could you pack a picnic lunch and head down to the beach with your family?

Relish in every day that God has graciously gifted you with. Instead of worrying about things that could go wrong in the future or beating yourself up over the past, consciously begin enjoying where you are and thank the Lord every day for it.

While all of these practical changes are helpful, the Christian carries an inner source of peace that others don't possess. We know as the Apostle said, that we can do *all* things through Him who gives us strength (Phil 4:13).

"All" means all of the work that God has required us to do. What stresses you out daily? Is it paying the bills, overcoming gossip, or meeting deadlines? Paul knew that He could be happy working meaningfully even if he had very little. And it wasn't because of his boundless strength. It was because he was strengthened by the One who is infinitely able. Before you wake up wondering how you're going to get through the day, turn to your Heavenly Father for what you need. He is always faithful.

## *The Benefits of Contentment*

Being content is more than just a good idea; it's critical to your overall well-being.

For starters, those who are content aren't always looking for material things to fill up their hearts and homes. So they learn to keep themselves busy with productive hobbies and projects. And they develop a healthier lifestyle.

Maybe, for example, you enjoy woodworking, reading, or biking. All of these can help with your mental acuity and physical fitness. This can boost your heart health, combat anxiety, and improve sleep quality. Being happy with what you've got can also help to strengthen your immune system and keep stress away.

If you want to live a long time and enjoy your time while you have it, contentment is key. Practice starting each day by counting your blessings rather than reminding yourself of what you don't have. Your body, mind, and soul will thank you for decades.

# Build on Where You Are

The phrase "bloom where you're planted" has often been used to encourage folks to celebrate and cultivate their current circumstances. Wishing you were someone or somewhere else is futile and disheartening. So is berating yourself about unwise decisions you've made in the past.

Instead, take an honest look at where you are and figure out how you can use it to your advantage. Embrace the mess. Seasons of financial lack can be wonderful opportunities for personal and professional growth. And they can make you infinitely more compassionate.

Do you want to pay off debt, save for the future, and get wiser with your spending?

Here's how you can begin building a future you can look forward to.

## *Pay Off Debt*

Believe it or not, 14 million Americans have more than $10,000 in credit card debt. If you're dealing with debt, you're not alone.

Most people don't go into debt intentionally. They may begin by charging necessities, such as a car or food, and are surprised at how quickly the tally and interest accumulate. Or they borrow in order to make an investment in their future, which is what happens with student loan debt or business loans. Before they know it, the bills become monsters that are always skulking in the shadows, even when they are having a good day.

If you have reasonable debts, such as a mortgage, making your required payment every month is smart. However, with dangerous debt such as credit cards and student loans, you'll eventually need to pay more than the minimum in order to get out from underneath the burden.

Before you begin to pay your debt down, you'll want to make an honest assessment of what you've actually got to pay off. While this can seem like a painful exercise at first, it can actually prove to be quite a relief when you're done. You'll know exactly what you're responsible for paying off in order to put yourself in an advantageous financial position. You're getting to know your monster, so you'll have a better chance of destroying it.

Besides credit cards and student loans, you'll also want to think about things like car loans, medical bills, and government debt. Make a list of your debt in the order of smallest to biggest.

While your mortgage technically qualifies as debt, there's no reason to include this in your debt total for the time being. Along with your taxes, utilities, and grocery bills, you can list this as a part of your daily living expenses.

The next step to financial liberation, of course, is to come up with a strategy for getting rid of what you owe. Some financial experts recommend paying off your smallest debt as quickly as possible, while you continue to pay the minimums on your other loans. This will give you some much-needed beginning success, and allow you to cut back on the number of creditors you have.

If you have the means, begin paying more than the minimum amount on your other loans as well. This will reduce your credit card utilization, which will in turn improve your credit score. It will also free up more of your credit for use in emergencies.

## Finding the Funds

Of course, paying off your debts in any order requires having the means to do it. This will demand a bit of discipline on your part that will pay off big dividends in the end.

One popular way to find the money you need is to find a second job or side hustle that can help increase your income. You may want to commit to using the money you make from this gig only for paying down debts. This can reassure you that whatever you're making in your primary job can still be used to cover your living expenses.

If you've got a family, it can be tricky to find the time to get out for work more often. Fortunately, today's world offers a number of remote jobs that you can tackle while your kids are completing their homework or enjoying their downtime. They include online bookkeeping, virtual tutoring, or customer service. Do a little research and figure out which opportunities would make the best use of your skills and interests. You'd be surprised at how many companies are looking for reliable employees to fill in part-time.

If you don't have little ones at home, you can feel free to pursue many different kinds of side gigs. You may be interested in real estate, babysitting, or professional photography. God has blessed each of us with skills we can use for His glory, as well as our own financial well-being. Figure out how you could arrange your schedule to take on extra work while still having time for the people and activities you love.

Another important way to get the money you need to pay down your debt is to make sure you've got a budget in place. Overspending or unnecessary expenses will be the quickest way to get yourself strapped into another ride on the debt spiral. We'll talk about this more in the next chapter.

## Build a Nest Egg

A "nest egg" has typically been referred to as money you've saved for retirement. You'll also need to make sure you're saving enough for your children's education if that's in your future.

Many experts agree that your retirement income should be about 80% of your pre-retirement income. This means you should have ten times your annual income saved by the time you are age 67. You may have a variety of income sources that include Social Security, pensions, and benefit plans. Many individuals also elect to work part-time in retirement in order to pay for expenses and stay active. It's important, however, to keep in mind that this isn't always possible.

Experts recommend saving 15% of your annual income beginning in your 20s so that you have a nice nest egg built up. Many individuals, however, don't begin thinking seriously about retirement until they are deeper into their working years.

If you work for an established company, you're probably eligible to begin saving through their retirement plan. Many employers will require that you contribute at least a minimum amount each month.

These plans are usually known as 401K, 403b, or 459 (b) plans. A traditional 401K plan will invest your money pre-tax, which will help you out by reducing your taxable income. A Roth 401K will take the money out of your income after tax, but your withdrawals will be free. You also won't pay any taxes on your money's growth.

If you haven't been saving 15% of your income, talk to your HR representative about how you can begin making bigger contributions. The amount you're legally allowed to save for retirement will increase after you turn 50.

Those who are self-employed or working part-time may need to begin building a nest egg without the help of their employer. If that's the case, you may need to find a broker who can help you find a smart traditional or Roth IRA, Solo 401K, or SEP-IRA to invest in. The right advisor can help you weigh the pros and cons of each type of account as they relate to your individual situation.

If you have children, you'll need to plan for their future as well. Your child may plan to begin working directly after high school or attend a trade school to get some skills before beginning a career.

If, however, your child plans on attending a four-year institution, it's recommended that at least one-third of this payment comes from savings and investments. Other ways to fund an education include financial aid, scholarships, and your income while your child is in school.

One of the most common ways to save for education is a 529 plan, which offers tax benefits and doesn't require much money to open. Experts recommend putting aside around $140 per child monthly if you're planning on sending them to an in-state public school and $350 per month if you're hoping to send your scholar to a private university.

You can also invest in your child's future through a Roth IRA, custodial account, or mutual funds. A great trusted financial advisor or certified accountant can help you make a smart decision.

## Starting a Business

Business loans can often be a tricky undertaking, but the right savings put aside can help you start up a company without owing anyone money.

Your first step should be to figure out what the start-up costs of your business will be. These include major equipment, office space, and inventory. You'll also want to think about licensing, employee salaries, and marketing.

Of course, there are ways to do all of these things economically when you're starting out. For example, you may be able to start your business from home, which can help you put off investing too much until you are turning a profit. Or you can invest in inexpensive social media marketing that can be tailored to your target audience.

Once you've figured out what you need, you can begin putting aside money each month to prepare for your enterprise. The right savings account with a good interest rate can help you save a nice chunk of change. It's then time to adjust your budget so that you're saving every month for your business.

## Don't Spend More Than You Have

Of course, one of the most fundamental ways to have enough money to pay off debts, save for the future, and fund a business is to avoid spending more money than you have. This is often easier said than done.

Take an honest look at your budget. Are there unnecessary things you're wasting money on?

For example, you can save up to $1,200 a year by making your coffee at home rather than picking it up at your local shop. And you can save almost the same amount by packing your lunch every day rather than eating out.

Making lists before you shop and reducing your social media scroll time can also help you resist the spending urge. The less you know about what you don't have, the better.

The best way to keep track of your spending is to have a family budget that's written down somewhere. This is an excellent discipline that will get easier as you practice it. And it may not be as difficult to follow as you think.

## Establish and Stick to a Budget

If you can create a simple spreadsheet on Google Docs or Microsoft Excel, you can establish a budget. You can also find plenty of readily-designed household budget templates online. Having a visible, written budget will help you to reign in your spending habits, invest monthly, and avoid disputes within your home.

Most families who budget do so monthly, but you can also set up one that runs bi-weekly or bi-monthly. The frequency of your income payments and bills can help you determine what's right for you.

The first step you'll need to take when creating a budget is to determine how much money you make within the budgeting period. This includes wages, child support payments, and income from side gigs.

The next column should list your daily living expenses. These include things like your mortgage or rent, taxes, and utility bills. You'll also want to budget for how much money you spend on food each week, including takeout if you eat it on a regular basis. Maybe you contribute money each month to a Health Savings Plan that helps you pay for medical bills. Or perhaps you have monthly self-care expenses, such as haircuts or dry cleaning bills. Of course, if your tithing is regular, include it in your budget plan.

Don't leave out anything that you spend money on regularly. You don't want to underestimate your spending, as this will give you an unrealistic idea of what you're going to have leftover at the end of every month.

Naturally, budgeting involves more than just keeping track of what you earn and spend. Once you figure out how much money you have and where it's going, you'll have to adjust your spending to make sure you have more cash left over.

If your goal is to pay down debt and/or build up a nest egg or save for college, create a separate column for how much you'd like to put aside for those things each month. The same holds true if you are saving money to start a business. Figure out how much you'll need to put aside each month in order to reach your goal, and adjust your budget accordingly.

You'll also want to put away a little each month for a "rainy day." This will probably mean that you'll need to shrink what you spend in your expense column.

Families can get really creative when it comes to cutting down on their costs. For example, you may be able to lower your energy bills by installing a programmable thermometer and using more warm clothes and blankets when the weather is cold. Weather-stripping windows and doors can also help you to avoid energy leaks.

If your family tends to use a lot of electricity, install "smart" power strips that will make sure you're only using energy when devices are on. You can also teach everyone to turn off the lights in rooms they aren't using.

If possible, spend time looking for digital coupons online or plan your weekly menu around what's on sale at your local grocery store. Getting the best prices might also mean that you'll need to switch to a different store or start buying generic brands.

Some people buy in bulk at big box stores in order to save money per unit. This can be a tremendous help if you have a big family, but you'll want to be careful to avoid impulse buys while you're there. Bulk buying means a lot will go to waste if you aren't going to use it!

If you look through your credit card bill each month, you may discover that there are certain money leaks you can plug up. For example, maybe you're spending money on apps or subscriptions you aren't using. Or maybe you can join a different gym for the fraction of the cost of your current fitness center.

Setting a budget is a discipline your children will remember as they get older. If you want everyone in your house to learn financial responsibility as a way of life, it's never too late to start budgeting.

## Sticking With It

While it's possible for most of us to create a beautifully balanced budget for our homes, it won't be worth anything if no one can stick with the plan.

Making lists before you shop, as well as knowing the price of what you're shopping for, will go a long way toward helping you avoid overspending when you're at the checkout counter. Take the time to list prices for the items you're planning on purchasing so there will be no surprises.

Some individuals use cash only when they shop so they are unable to spend more than they have. Others find it helps to have only one credit card so they know exactly what they have to pay off each month.

Most of today's budgeting tools are digital, which means you can access them from anywhere if you've got a phone. One way to keep better track of your money is to make notes of everything digitally when you make purchases at, for example, the grocery store or coffee shop.

How much do you have budgeted for food this month, and how much of that will be gone if you make this purchase? Keeping your budget in front of you at all times can ensure that you aren't making foolish decisions.

If you have kids, talk to them about your budget when you're out at the store and when you're "reconciling" it at home by checking it against your bank account and credit card.

Once you've saved up some money, let your spouse and/or children see the results whether it's in a jar or bankbook. If it helps you stay with the plan, reward everyone with something small each month just for hanging in there, such as a day at the movies. Eventually, sticking with your budget will become something that everyone expects to do and takes pride in.

# Helping Your Family Set Limits

There's no doubt that today's kids are savvy when it comes to shopping. Everyone knows a cute story like the one about the four-year-old who ordered a dollhouse on Amazon and had it shipped to the house before her parents even knew about the purchase.

Teaching your family to set limits on spending can help their character to develop. With the right guidance, your children will be unspoiled and learn the value of hard work and saving when it comes to financial success.

## Practical Tips

The less your children are showered with indulgences, the more they will appreciate it when they are treated to them once in a while. For example, teach your children to enjoy the simplicity of meals at home. You can let them help you out in the kitchen while you're playing their favorite music. They can even assist with things like meal planning and coupon-clipping. Save take-out and restaurant visits as special rewards that happen once or twice a month.

If you don't have the means to purchase expensive clothes, help your little one to find great outfits at thrift shops or discount stores. Hand-me-downs are smart because the price is right, and you can still allow junior to pick out a few new items to complement them. Chances are that your little ones will only be wearing the clothes for a single season anyway since they are always growing.

Many children love to go shopping for toys, clothes, or sweets when you go out for necessities. If you're a busy parent, you may want to get out to the store without them or shop online so you don't end up purchasing things you don't need in order to avoid a public disagreement.

If your child is a bit older, allow them to get an age-appropriate job so they can learn the value of earning what they spend. For example, a 12-year-old can do yard work, get a paper route, walk dogs or even get paid to do household chores. Your 15-year-old may be able to babysit, become a grocery store bagger work in a restaurant a carwash be a cashier or even a caddy at a golf club.

Many tweens and teens enjoy the independence of being able to earn their own money and spend it at their discretion. However, they will also get a tangible lesson in how many hours they need to work in order to afford things such as video games or a new pair of jeans. A part-time job can provide your children with a newfound gratitude for your sacrifices, as well as pride in their own accomplishments.

## *Saving, Spending, and Tithing*

Left to themselves, most young people would choose to spend all of their earnings. However, responsible parents teach them the value of saving and tithing early on.

Many parents teach this principle to younger children by splitting allowances or gifts into jars. This provides a visible representation of how they are stewarding their resources. As children get older, you may want to use envelopes or a spreadsheet to help them learn to divide their earnings responsibly.

These parents teach children to give their tithe (see chapter two), 10% of whatever they receive to the Lord. This is a habit they will not depart from if they learn it early. They may choose to put it toward a Sunday School offering or give it to their favorite Christian charity.

The next jar should be for savings. Many experts recommend that children save around 25%. If your child is motivated by big purchases, ask them to pick out something that they would really love to own as a goal for their savings. It could be a bike, video game system, or pair of roller skates. Your child will be quite proud when they are able to purchase it with their own money by staying disciplined for an extended period of time. As your child gets older, they may want to save for things like a car or books for college.

The remaining jar is 65% that can be spent. If your child is younger, a pack of gum or a small toy may be all it takes to make them happy. Older children may prefer using their spending money for things like gourmet coffee with friends or personal care products.

Whether your child is earning an allowance or working a small job, teach them to enjoy the fruits of their labor responsibly through spending, saving, and tithing. Those who continue this habit throughout their lives will always be grateful for what you taught them.

## *Setting Limits is Stewardship*

When it comes to setting limits, there are two main reasons: one is that only by spending less than you make can you ever build savings. It's simple math and so easy in theory to do, but the vast majority of humanity has almost no savings, because we are unable to set limits for ourselves.

The other main reason we must help our family set limits is that it creates self-discipline. Our whole lives are dedicated to stewardship (see chapter ten), and if we don't set limits, we cannot possibly manage what God has given us. Setting limits is the essence of stewardship. Stewards must allocate resources, and since our resources in the short term are limited, we must submit to reality. The failure to set limits is the failure to accept the truth of how things are. We must know our limits and then stick to them. We must teach our children to do the same.

# Break the Family Debt Curse

It's possible for children to inherit debt from their parents after they pass, but it's more likely that a parent's debts will be paid through the sale of their home or other assets. More often than not, children suffer in the sense that they are denied inheritances because their parents were not careful with their money. They don't have the benefit of the funds they could have used for the funeral or future expenses. Those elders who pass down the profits from homes or savings accounts to their children give them a real advantage.

The exception would be if you co-signed a loan or got a joint credit card with your parents, in which case you will be responsible for paying whatever is owed. Before agreeing to borrow money with an older family member, make sure you know what their spending habits are like, and if they will be able to pay off what they owe.

The curse of family debt will more than likely get bestowed on future generations through poor financial habits that are learned and passed down. For example, someone may see their parents buying on impulse even when the price isn't right or refuse to create a budget. These are the kinds of patterns that are easy to learn. Yet breaking them is not as difficult as it may seem.

## Breaking Bad Habits

In some families, money is rarely talked about, which may give children the impression that the topic is shameful. Worse still, they may get the idea that having enough money for everything they want is easy and learn to become unwise spenders.

Most of today's schools don't teach financial planning. This is why it's critical for parents to have honest, healthy conversations with their children about good habits. They will learn that money is something they can get control of and use for their benefit.

Talk to your kids about saving and tithing, and provide them with plenty of visuals if they are young. As they get older, you can talk to them about things like how much you're saving for college and why you aren't making big purchases like an expensive car or a boat.

Show your kids how to have a meaningful life that involves hobbies and friends rather than spending money. For example, encourage them to read a book, practice an instrument, or call a friend the next time they want to go shopping. Explain that you will treat them to a special purchase sometime, but it may have to be earned. For example, you might buy them a new toy if they get all As on their report card.

If you feel unqualified to talk to your kids about financial matters, don't give up! Find a member of your church who would be willing to sit down with your family and help you to create a basic financial plan. Involve your children in the discussion so they can take pride in their contribution to the family.

Kid-friendly books and websites on saving and spending God's way are always available. As a parent, don't be afraid to reach out to provide some solid guidance to your kids. This will put them at a real advantage as they become young adults with their own careers, families, and dreams.

## Sowing and Reaping

One of the most important laws parents can teach their children is the Biblical principle of sowing and reaping. Galatians 6:7-9 tells us that "Do not be deceived; God is not mocked, for whatever one sows, that will he also reap. For the one who sows to his own flesh will from the flesh reap corruption, but the one who sows to the Spirit will from the Spirit reap eternal life. And do not weary of doing good, for in due season we will reap, if we do not give up" (ESV).

This is a serious word that we should impart to our children if we care about them. In life, they will get out whatever they put in.

For example, if your children don't make an effort to be kind to their friends, they aren't going to have many. And if they aren't behaving at school, they shouldn't expect teachers to shower praise on them.

The same principle applies to finances. If your child is spending all of their money on whatever they please, "sowing to their flesh," they should not expect a good return. Instead, they should focus on saving, tithing, and glorifying God with their resources.

Let your child catch you modeling good behavior such as putting money in a church envelope, opening a savings account, or sponsoring a child in another country. They will learn to see these activities as right and joyful. The child who follows God's laws when it comes to their money will reap an impressive harvest as long as they don't give up.

# Salvation and Stewardship

Proverbs 5:23 tells us that "he dies from lack of discipline, and because of his great folly he is led astray" (ESV).

A refusal to discipline yourself can cost you your very life. Salvation is a free gift from Jesus, but not honoring God with your finances can cause you great pain in this present world. It also does not set a good example for those around you.

## The Meaning of Stewardship

The dictionary describes stewardship as "the conducting, supervising, or managing of something."

As Christians, we know that Jesus will be returning one day. Yet before He does, He expects us to take good care of the things we have been entrusted with on His behalf.

1 Peter 4:10 tells us "As each has received a gift, use it to serve one another, as good stewards of God's varied grace" (ESV).

Many of us feel called to make good use of our talents and spiritual gifts. We would sense that we wouldn't be honoring the God who saved us if we let these things go to waste. Yet God has also gifted you with financial resources that you need to use wisely. This is integral to your financial stability as well as the economic well-being of future generations.

The first step in becoming a good steward is to acknowledge, inwardly and outwardly, that the resources you have are not ultimately yours, but God's. He gave you the arms and brains to work with and placed you in a free society where you are able to earn an honorable wage. Your heavenly Father expects you to make good use of these advantages, and He will hold you accountable.

## Freedom in Serving

Another major step toward becoming an excellent steward is to get rid of your debt. As we discussed in previous chapters, this requires a plan and extra discipline on your part. You can then begin to tithe, save, and pass on good financial principles to your children. These are important aspects of pleasing God with your money.

Perhaps, however, you haven't been a good steward of your finances up to this point. Rest assured that God has not abandoned you. Your Heavenly Father loves you and wants you to succeed. Begin seeking Him for guidance with financial planning, extra employment, or starting a business. Ask him to bring godly people and opportunities into your life that will support and encourage you.

If your intention is to honor your Father through your financial turnaround, He can and will help you. You can then strengthen others through what you have learned.

The Bible tells us "So, whether you eat or drink, or whatever you do, do it all to the glory of God" (1 Cor 10:31, ESV).

God has given you gifts and opportunities that no one else has had or ever will again. Allow your heart to glorify God in all of your undertakings. You will be amazed at what He can do with whatever you've got to give.

## *The Devil's Trap*

Debt is a curse. Satan loves for us to be in debt, and he especially loves to see Christians in debt. It is a trap he has used for centuries. He loves any sort of bondage, and he excels in getting God's children to fall into this particular trap. But Satan has no real power if you will make the decision today to take it away from him. Submit yourself to God and His ways. If you will follow what God teaches in His Word about money and stewardship, you will frustrate the Devil. Any day that Satan doesn't get his way is a good day.

My prayer for you is that you will absorb these lessons for yourself, for your children, and for your children's children. I pray God's blessing and favor on your stewardship of the time, talent, money and resources He has entrusted you with. I pray that you will go to Him one day to show Him what you have done with what He has given you, and He will say, "Well done! Good and faithful servant! Come and share in the joy of your Master" (Mt 25:21)!

# ABOUT THE AUTHOR

Phyllis Tufts Hightower was raised in a small town in Georgia. While growing up her parents laid the foundation for her Christian faith. After graduating from college and while working as a mental health professional she was called to ministry. Phyllis is a wife and mother, who for over 20 years has been a prolific teacher of the Word of God.

She currently serves in ministry as an Elder, Adult Bible Teacher and Sunday School Superintendent. She has traveled to many countries including Haiti and Africa. Her goal has been to spread the gospel and to teach that financial freedoms are not limited by one's circumstances but by a lack of understanding in the truth of God's word. It is her hope that this book will help people live a debt free life.

Printed in the United States
by Baker & Taylor Publisher Services